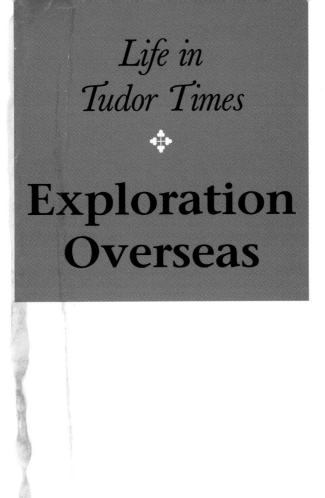

Life in
Tudor Times

✥

Exploration
Overseas

Jane Shuter

First published in Great Britain by Heinemann Library
Halley Court, Jordan Hill, Oxford OX2 8EJ
a division of Reed Educational and Professional Publishing Ltd

OXFORD FLORENCE PRAGUE MADRID ATHENS
MELBOURNE AUCKLAND KUALA LUMPUR SINGAPORE TOKYO
IBADAN NAIROBI KAMPALA JOHANNESBURG GABORONE
PORTSMOUTH NH (USA) CHICAGO MEXICO CITY SAO PAULO

Typeset by Getset
Illustrations by Hardlines: pages 4 & 6; Oxford Illustrators: pages 10–11
Printed in Great Britain by Bath Press Colourbooks, Glasgow

00 99 98 97 96
10 9 8 7 6 5 4 3 2 1

ISBN 0 431 06758 9 (This title is also available in a hardback edition ISBN 0 431 06757 0)

British Library Cataloguing in Publication Data
Shuter, Jane
   Exploration overseas. – (Life in Tudor times)
   1. Discoveries in geography – Juvenile literature 2. England
   – Discovery and exploration – Juvenile literature 3. Great
   Britain – History – Tudors, 1485–1603 – Juvenile literature
   I. Title
   910.9'42

Acknowledgements
The Publishers would like to thank the following for permission to reproduce photographs.
Bodleian Library: p.19; Bridgeman Art Library: p.17, p.21, p.25, p.29; British Library: p.9; British
Museum: p.13, p.23; Michael Holford/British Museum: p.15; Michael Holford/National Maritime
Museum: p.11; National Maritime Museum Picture Library: p.5, p.7, p.14, p.16, p.27; National
Portrait Gallery: p.18.

Cover photograph reproduced with the permission of The National Portrait Gallery.

Our thanks to Dr Michael Mullett, of the Department of History at Lancaster University, for his
comments in the preparation of this book.

Every effort has been made to contact copyright holders of any material reproduced in this book.
Any omissions will be rectified in subsequent printings if notice is given to the Publisher.

Details of written sources
Joel Hurstfield & Alan G R Smith, *Elizabethan People, State & Society*, Edward Arnold 1972: Source B,
page 13
Neville Williams, *Francis Drake*, Weidenfeld & Nicholson 1973: Source D, page 14: Source E, page
14; Source H, page 16
Neville Williams, *Elizabeth 1*, Weidenfeld & Nicholson 1975: Source G, page 16
The Great Age of Exploration, Reader's Digest 1971: Source A, page 4; Source B, page 7; Source A,
page 10
The Roanoke Voyages, Hakluyt Society 1955: Source A, page 20; source B, page 20; Source D, page
22; Source E, page 22; Source H, page 25; Source I, page 26; Source K, page 28

CONTENTS

1 An age of discovery

During the Tudor period, from 1485 to 1603, European sailors made many dangerous **voyages** of exploration. So Europeans in 1603 knew more about the world than Europeans in 1485 (see maps below). Why did they go exploring? Very few people went just to find out what was there. There were two main reasons – religion and money.

Religion

All Europeans were **Christians**. They wanted to spread the Christian religion to other parts of the world. They wanted to reach new lands before the Arabs, who were also exploring and spreading their religion. The Arabs were **Muslims**, not Christians.

Source **A**

We come in search of Christians and spices.

Said by Vasco de Gama when he was asked by a **native** of Madagascar why he had come so far from Portugal. Trade and persuading people to become Christians were the main reasons all European nations went exploring.

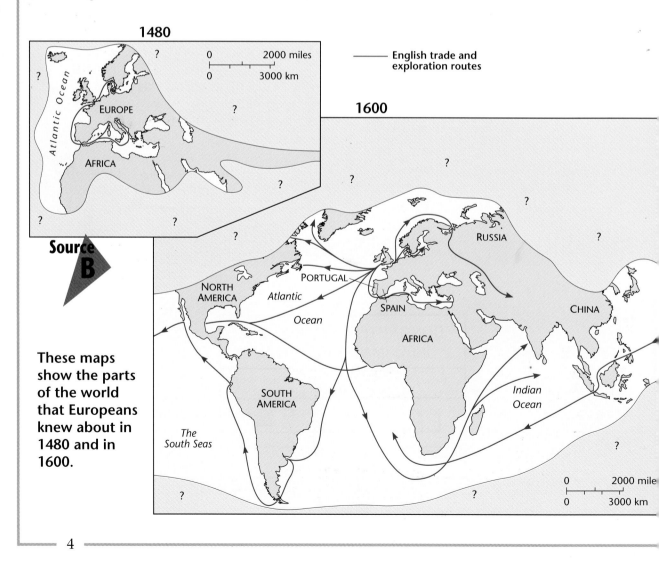

1480

? — English trade and exploration routes

Atlantic Ocean

EUROPE

AFRICA

1600

Source **B**

These maps show the parts of the world that Europeans knew about in 1480 and in 1600.

NORTH AMERICA

Atlantic Ocean

PORTUGAL

SPAIN

AFRICA

RUSSIA

CHINA

Indian Ocean

SOUTH AMERICA

The South Seas

0 — 2000 miles
0 — 3000 km

Trade

Merchants in Europe made a lot of money from **trade**. They wanted to find new countries to trade with or an easier way to reach countries they already knew about, like China and Asia, which they called 'the **Indies**'. **Monarchs** also supported explorations, as they hoped to claim new land for their country, or to make money from trade. Then the Spanish discovered South America and another reason to go exploring – gold and silver. They said the land belonged to Spain, so they could just take the gold and silver, not trade for it.

Who went?

A person could not just decide to go exploring. They needed properly equipped ships and enough sailors and **provisions** for the journey. These cost a lot of money. Very few people could afford to set up their own expeditions. They needed the help of someone rich who was prepared to take the risk of losing all their money if the ships sank or found nothing. Merchants and monarchs were the most likely people to set up expeditions.

Ships Trading in the East, painted by a Dutch artist, Hendrik Vroom, in 1614. English, Spanish, French and Dutch ships are arriving to trade in the same port. This would not have happened in real life, because these countries competed for trade. Spices from the Indies were especially valuable. Europeans used spices to stop their food going bad.

2 Early explorations

The first European explorers were Portuguese. The Portuguese **monarchs** wanted to find a sea route to the **Indies**, so most voyages were along the African coast. In 1495, Vasco da Gama rounded the southern tip of Africa and crossed the Indian Ocean.

Dividing up the world

At first, the Portuguese had no rivals. Then the Spanish monarchs helped Christopher Columbus to explore westwards, hoping to find the Indies before the Portuguese. When Columbus found the Caribbean islands in 1492, the Portuguese began to worry. Maybe there was a westward route to the Indies. They asked the **Pope**, head of the **Catholic** Church, for help. Spain and Portugal, both Catholic countries, had to obey the Pope. He said they had to share the unknown world. The Treaty of Tordesillias, signed in 1494, said where the dividing line was.

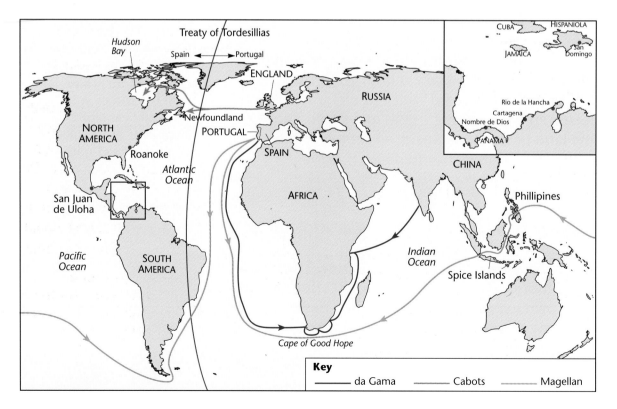

Portuguese Carracks off a Rocky Coast, painted by an unknown artist in 1540. **Carracks** were heavy (1,000 tons) and hard to steer. Explorers preferred smaller **caravels** (100 tons), which were easier to steer.

Around the world

The Portuguese concentrated on the eastward Indies route. They turned down the explorer Magellan's offer to find a western route. Spain agreed to help. In 1519 Magellan set out with five ships. It was winter by the time he reached St Julian. He decided to spend winter there. There was a **mutiny**. Magellan executed the ringleaders.

Three ships were seaworthy enough to round the southern point of South America and reach the Philippines. Here they were attacked by the **natives**. Magellan was among those killed. Only one ship made it home, but now people knew it was possible to reach the Indies by sailing west. They could sail around the world!

Source B

He could endure hunger better than anyone. He had a better understanding of sea charts and navigation than any man alive. Only he had the skill and courage to circumnavigate the world, as he would have had he got home.

Said by Antonio Pigafetta, an Italian sailor who sailed with Magellan in 1519.

3 England starts exploring

Henry VII and the Cabots

Henry VII was the first Tudor king. He wanted England to have good trade links with as many other countries as possible. John Cabot, an Italian **navigator** who lived in Bristol, told Henry that he was sure it was possible to reach the **Indies** by sailing north from England. He said this north-west passage would be quicker and cheaper than the land route (see map on page 6). In 1496, Henry VII gave Cabot letters allowing him and his son to explore and claim new land for England.

In 1497 the Cabots found and explored the coast of Newfoundland, but did not find a passage to the Indies. John made a second voyage in 1498, but never came back. His son, Sebastian, continued the search, finding Hudson Bay in 1508, but never finding the north-west passage.

The monarchs lose interest

Henry VIII, the next king, had no time for exploration. The importance of the Cabots' discoveries was not understood at the time. They had not found the Indies, nor any other rich foreign lands. Henry VIII could not see the point of another voyage. He was more concerned with not upsetting the Spanish by going exploring. He would rather spend his money on fighting the French.

Further exploration

Tudor **merchants** were still interested in exploration. They wanted to find new ways to the Indies, new places to trade with. They set up expeditions to find a north-west passage and one to the north-east. Their efforts were finally rewarded when they made contacts and **trade** links with Russia in 1553, but they never reached the Indies.

Source A

This engraving is from an account of William Barent's Dutch expedition north, printed in 1598. Northern exploration was the most dangerous of all. Ships were trapped in the ice, there were attacks by polar bears and Eskimos, and the weather was awful.

English expeditions to find a northwards passage

1497	Cabots go north-west, reach Newfoundland.
1498	John Cabot goes north-west, ships lost.
1508	Sebastian Cabot goes north-west, finds Hudson Bay.
1553	Willoughby and Chancellor go north-east, Willoughby lost. Chancellor makes trade links with Russia.
1576/7/8	Martin Frobisher goes north-west, reaches Hudson Bay, but is forced back by bad weather three times.
1580	Pet and Jackman go north-west, Jackman lost, Pet and crew almost die from exposure.
1585/6/7	Davis goes north-west, forced back by bad weather three times.

4 A sailor's life

Conditions on board

Explorers from all countries used the best ships that they could get. The best ships for long-distance sea voyages were **caravels**. They were small, fast and easy to steer. They were not used for trade, as they could not carry enough cargo. But they were better than **carracks** for exploration. All the space below deck was used to store food and drink, firewood to cook with, sails and ropes. The crew of about 30 men had to sleep on deck.

Food and drink

Sailors usually had one meal a day, a hot one, cooked on deck. They had to take enough food and drink with them to last the whole **voyage**. They took some fresh food, but most of their food was salted fish and meat and hard baked biscuits. These things kept for longer. They ate the fresh food first, then lived on the salted food. Often rats and **maggots** got to the food before the sailors did. They took barrels of water and wine. But the water soon turned bad and the wine went sour.

It was hard to keep clean on board. Sailors seldom washed or changed their clothes. They were often covered in **lice**. Because sailors got very little fresh food, especially vegetables, they often had a disease called **scurvy** from lack of **vitamin** C. They also caught other **diseases** easily and these spread quickly on such small ships. Not all ships had doctors. Even when there was a doctor on board there was very little he could do to help anyone, for no-one knew what caused diseases such as scurvy.

Source A

We ate crumbs of sea biscuit all full of **weevils** and stinking of rat urine. We drank yellowish water that was putrid. We ate cow **hides** and paid money for rats to eat.

Written by Antonio Pigafetta, who sailed with Magellan in 1519. He wrote this about four months after they left Spain.

Source B

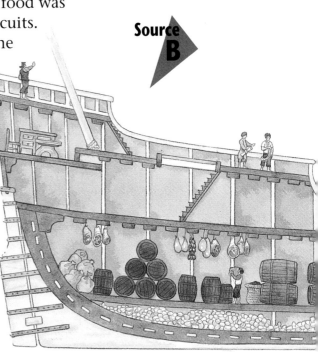

Daily work

The crew were divided into two groups, called watches. They took it in turns to work for four hours then rest for four hours. Each watch started by pumping the water out of the ship, because all wooden ships leak. They changed and mended the sails, mended holes in the ship, kept watch for land, storms, enemy ships or other dangers. They worked out how fast the ship was sailing. They checked the direction as best they could.

Source C

A compass from the 1500s. A compass works by using a magnet to find magnetic north. Sailors had used magnetic ore to navigate for hundreds of years.

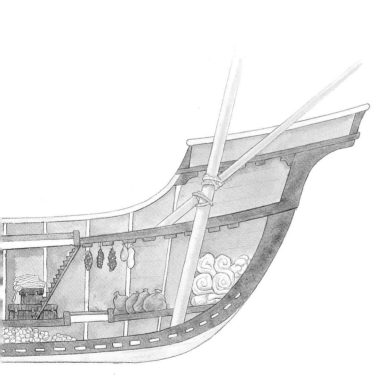

A modern drawing of a ship in about 1500. The space below deck, above where the food is stored, was the gun deck.

Finding your way

The navigational instruments sailors used were not very accurate, and they did not have accurate maps of where they were going to. They had no way of knowing how wide the Atlantic and Pacific oceans were. The only sea they knew well was the Mediterranean. The most common navigational instruments were:

- **a compass** – this pointed north.
- **a traverse board** – this was a pegboard with strings on it. Sailors used it to record their journey so they could retrace their route.
- **a quadrant** – this told the sailors where they were in relation to the equator.

5 Sir Francis Drake 1544–96

Early years

Francis Drake was born in Devon, but left in 1549. His family ended up living in a boat on the River Medway, in Kent. Francis went to sea when he was about ten, working for a **pilot** who guided ships up and down the rivers Medway and Thames. They also sailed along the English coast, taking fish from Yarmouth to London, and even going to Holland and France for wine, brandy and cheeses.

The pilot died in 1561 and left the ship to Francis. He decided to save money, sell his ship and join his relatives, the Hawkins family, in Plymouth. They were making money by **privateering** and **trade**. They took **slaves** from Africa to South America and sold them to the Spanish. Spanish **colonies** were told not to trade with the English, but they did.

First trading voyages

Drake's first Caribbean **voyage** for the Hawkins family was in 1566. The Spanish were now forcing their colonies not to trade with other countries. The English had to give away slaves they took to the Caribbean to sell.

In 1567 another expedition set out to sell slaves to the Spanish in the Caribbean. John Hawkins was in charge. Drake was captain of a ship for this voyage. The Spanish refused to trade. Hawkins took over the town, forced a trade and demanded a **ransom** for the town. He did this in other places, too. They had just taken San Juan de Ulhoa when a huge Spanish fleet arrived and a battle started. Drake, thinking his was the last ship, left as soon as night fell. He left Hawkins and one more small ship behind, with over a hundred men on board. They reached home several weeks after Drake. Some people said Drake had deliberately deserted Hawkins. Hawkins thought this, too, at first. He forgave Drake, but Drake did not sail for the family again. He started again, working for other **merchants**.

Source A

This is part of a painting of Great Yarmouth, made in about 1585. It was one of the places Drake would have visited as a boy on his trading trips.

England once had a hundred ships to defend the country. Queen Elizabeth can afford about fifteen. She has to rely on privateers. They make sure of ministers' support by giving them a share of the profit but not the expense of the voyage.

Written in 1602 by an Italian ambassador to England, to explain why privateering was not stopped.

Privateering

Privateers attacked ships from other countries and captured the ships, the crew and the cargo. This sounds like stealing. At the time it was seen as helping your country. Even when countries were not at war, raids on other countries' ships were accepted by the government – as long as they got some of the loot! Many captains saw privateering as part of any voyage – and the best way to make a profit.

Source C

Drake's dial, a navigational instrument made especially for Drake. He needed a portable set of instruments, because he was travelling by sea and on land.

Revenge!

By 1571 Drake had enough money to return to the Caribbean by himself. He mapped the coastline around Panama, where the Spanish carried silver overland from their **mines** to the sea. He was shown the Pacific, and swore to cross it one day. He hid **supplies** in a sheltered bay. Then he went home to plan. In 1573 Drake returned to Panama to raid the Spanish treasure house at Nombre de Dios.

Things began disastrously. Drake's men captured Nombre de Dios, but the treasure house was empty and Drake was badly wounded. A **donkey train** carrying silver avoided his ambush. Drake did not go home. He stayed and his luck changed. He captured silver carried overland, and gold at sea – worth £320,000. (A craftworker made about £10 a year.)

Ireland

When Drake returned to England in 1574, the Queen was close to signing a peace treaty with Spain, so Drake could not set out to the Caribbean again. Instead, hoping to please the Queen, he joined the English army fighting in Ireland.

Source D

If it pleases God that I should reach my frigate then, by one means or another, I will get you all aboard too, in spite of all the Spaniards in the Indies.

Said by Drake to his men while trying to reach the English ships at Nombre de Dios on a raft made from some wood and a biscuit sack. The raft was often completely under water in the rough sea, but Drake believed they would be safe. His confidence in times of danger gave his sailors confidence, too.

Source E

He is a man of about 35 years, short, with a fair beard. He is one of the greatest sailors ever, both as a **navigator** and a commander. He treats his men with affection and they treat him with respect. He shows them great favour, but punishes the least fault.

Said by Francisco de Zarate, a Spanish captain captured by Drake in 1578.

Source F

This Flemish map, printed in 1589, was the first to show Drake's route around the world.

Around the world

By 1577, England and Spain were enemies again. The Queen gave Drake permission for a voyage. We do not know if she knew he planned to go around the world. He certainly did not tell the sailors. One of the sailors was Thomas Doughty, a friend of Drake's from Ireland.

The voyage began badly. By the time they reached the southern point of South America, Drake had to leave three ships as unseaworthy. There was almost a mutiny among the unhappy sailors, started by Doughty.

Drake held a trial. Doughty was found guilty and chose to be executed rather than be left behind or sent back to England as a prisoner.Three ships crossed into the Pacific. They were hit by a storm. One was lost. Another was blown off course and returned to England, where the crew said that Drake's ship, the *Pelican* (re-named the *Golden Hind*), was lost too. But it was not. After the storm, Drake was more successful. In 1580 he returned. He had seized Spanish gold, claimed California for England and set up trade with Ternate, one of the Spice Islands.

Sir Francis Drake

Drake was now famous and popular. He was also very rich. He kept treasure worth £10,000. The crew were given the same amount to share. The Queen took most of the rest, about £300,000. She knighted Drake and gave him land. He was elected Mayor of Portsmouth and **MP** for Portsmouth. Bad things also happened. Mary Drake, his wife, died. John Doughty accused Drake of murdering his brother, Thomas, which did Drake's reputation no good.

In 1585 Drake was back at sea. Philip II of Spain had ordered the arrest of English merchants living and trading in Spain and Portugal. Drake was sent to get the merchants safely home and then attack the Spanish in the Caribbean. The merchants refused to leave Spain and Portugal so he left them. In the Caribbean Drake took San Domingo and Cartagena, important Spanish towns, but sickness broke out on the ships, so they headed for home.

Raiding Spain

In 1587 Drake set out to fight the Spanish again – this time in Spain. Elizabeth had heard that the Spanish were preparing a huge invasion fleet. Drake was sent to find out what was going on, and to stop it. Then the Queen changed her mind. She sent orders to Drake not to attack Spain. Drake had already sailed. A ship was sent after him with the message. He said it never arrived. Some people said it arrived but he ignored it.

Source G

You shall not enter any of the King's ports by force, nor offer any violence to his towns or shipping.

Part of the message sent by Elizabeth I to Drake, which he said never arrived.

Source H

Drake has done so much damage to the coast of Spain that even if the King captured Drake he would not recover one half of what he has lost.

Written by a French visitor to Spain in 1587. Drake's success explains why the Queen did not ask why he did not get her message. She ignored disobedience, as long as she benefited from it. Drake was less lucky in 1589.

Source I

The sea chest Drake took on his voyages. When Drake became rich he lived well at sea. This was, at least in part, to impress those he captured. The Spaniard, de Zarate, captured in 1578, said, 'He travels with all possible luxuries.'

Drake's raid on Spain was totally unexpected and very successful. He captured six warships and sunk 31. He also captured Philip II's own treasure ship loaded with spices, silk and gold worth £114,000.

The Armada and after

Drake was one of the commanders in the English fleet that drove off the Spanish Armada in 1588. He then set off on another raid on Spain in 1589. This was a failure. Many men and ships were lost. Nothing was gained. Drake was held to blame for this, and for a long time Elizabeth I would not let him sail again. He stayed quietly in Devon with his new wife.

At last, in 1595, the Queen sent Drake and John Hawkins to the Caribbean. The ships were struck by fever early in the voyage. Hawkins died. Drake took Rio de la Hancha and Nombre de Dios. But he, too, caught the fever and died, on 28 June 1695. He was buried at sea in a lead coffin in Nombre de Dios Bay.

Source J

Sir Francis Drake, painted in 1591 by an unknown artist. The sword is to show he is a gentleman. The globe is to remind us of his exploration.

A good captain?

There were ways in which Drake was a good captain. There were ways in which he was not. Accounts given by men who sailed with him say he was brave and fearless, that he worked as hard on board as any of the men and that the ordinary seamen 'adored him'.

Others said he was too quick to lead everyone into danger, always took too many sailors on board (increasing the risks of infection) and was not good at managing a fleet and the captains under him.

6   Sir Walter Raleigh 1554–1618

Childhood and youth

Like Drake, Walter Raleigh was born in Devon, but his early life was very different. He was born into a **noble** family. His family was not rich, but he did not have to work for a living. Instead he went to **Court** and became one of the many young men Queen Elizabeth I chose to favour.

Life at Court

Raleigh fitted in well at Court in some ways. He was handsome, clever and good at dancing, poetry, writing and hunting. He was also a soldier and fought in Ireland in 1580. From 1582 he was one of Elizabeth I's favourites. She gave him land in England and Ireland and also presents of money and important jobs at Court. Raleigh became proud and boastful. Many courtiers came to dislike him.

Source
B

He was handsome and well built. He had a good wit and a bold plausible tongue that could turn his good reading to his advantage. On his second Irish **voyage** he disagreed with Lord Grey and argued his case so well to the Queen and her Council that he quickly got the Queen's ear.

From *Fragmenta Regalia*, written by Robert Naunton in 1641. Naunton lived in Elizabeth's Court and wrote a description of the Queen and the important people of her reign.

Source
A

Raleigh, painted in 1588 by Zuccero.

Voyage to the New World

Source C

In 1584 Raleigh put money into a voyage of exploration to North America. He had been granted the right to explore there. He did not go himself, but sent two experienced captains, Armadas and Barlowe. They found land, which Raleigh named Virginia, and came back saying the land was good and the **natives** were friendly. They brought home two native Indians and plants, including potato and tobacco plants. The Indians and tobacco were a huge success. A **colony** at Roanoke was planned. The story of this colony is told on pages 20–29. Raleigh was knighted in 1585.

An illustration of the potato plant, taken from John Gerarde's *Herball*, printed in 1597.

Disgrace

In 1592 one of the Queen's ladies-in-waiting gave birth to a son. To the delight of Raleigh's enemies it became clear that she had married Raleigh secretly some years before, but they had kept the marriage a secret to avoid upsetting the Queen. Elizabeth was furious. She hated secrecy and did not like her favourites to marry. She had Raleigh imprisoned in the Tower of London. She eventually let him out, but he was never a favourite again.

El Dorado

Source D

In 1595 Raleigh set out on an expedition to South America, looking for an ancient city, El Dorado, which was rich in gold. He found Guyana instead. He came home and wrote an account of the journey.

In 1603 Elizabeth I died. Her successor, James I, was sure that Raleigh had plotted against him, so he put him in the Tower until 1616. He was allowed to return to South America to search for El Dorado, if he did not upset the Spanish there. When the ships arrived, Raleigh was too ill to go ashore. His son, also Walter, was one of those that went. They got into a fight with some Spaniards. Walter was killed. Raleigh sailed home. He was put in prison for fighting the Spanish, and executed in 1618.

Say to the Court it glows
And shines like rotten wood,
Say to the Church it shows
What's good but does no
    good. . .
Tell men of high condition
That manage the estate,
Their purpose is ambition
Their practice only hate.

Part of a poem written by Raleigh in about 1605. He is bitter about the Court and courtiers, the men of 'high condition' who run England ('the estate' in the poem).

7   The Roanoke colony

First views of Roanoke

On 27 April 1584, two ships left Plymouth, sailing
for North America. Walter Raleigh sent them to see
if it would be a good place to settle. On 4 July they
saw land. On 13 July they sailed along the coast and
met some Indians who were fishing. The Indians
were friendly. Soon the sailors were visiting the
Indians and studying the land and the people.

By September they were back in England. They said
they had found a beautiful place, where animals
were plentiful and crops grew well. They brought
samples of the local plants, including potatoes and
tobacco, and two Indians, Manteo and Wanchese.
Everyone was told the voyage had been a success and
Roanoke, as they named it, was a good place to
colonize.

The whole truth?

We now have evidence from the time that suggests
that most people were only told the good things
about the expedition. Some things that might put
people off going to set up a **colony** were left out.
- There may have been a landing party sent ashore
  before Roanoke. A survivor of the **voyage** said
  there was: they were killed and eaten by Indians.
- Two Englishmen may have been left at Roanoke as
  hostages for Manteo and Wanchese, not a sign of
  perfect trust by the Indians. If so, they were never
  heard of again. If they had been alive when the
  second expedition arrived, the colonists would
  have mentioned them.
- There was no mention that the government
  intended to use the colony as a **military base**
  against the Spanish living further south, in Florida.
  This was why so many soldiers went on the second
  expedition to Roanoke, in 1585, and why they
  quickly built a **fort**. The soldiers and the fort were
  part of the reason for the failure of the second
  expedition.

Source A

This Island has
woods full of deer,
rabbits and hares.
There are cedars and
cinnamon trees. The
soil is plentiful, sweet
and wholesome. We
put some of our pea
seeds into it and in ten
days they were fourteen
inches high. We found
the people gentle,
loving and truthful.

**Written by Arthur
Barlowe on his return
from Roanoke in 1584.**

Source B

Barlowe wanted to
land first in one place.
But the wild Indians
killed and ate 38
Englishmen, so they
moved on to the next
place, where the savages
were more gentle. Here
they traded and took
back two Indians,
leaving two Englishmen
so that they would
return.

**An Englishman,
questioned by the
Spanish in Jamaica in
1586, said he had been
part of the expedition.
This was part of his
story of the voyage.**

Colonizing new lands

The **monarch** of a country gave someone (usually **noble** and rich) letters that gave them permission to explore, settle, **trade** with and take over a certain area. They gave the person control over places that could be very profitable.

The first grant for English exploration around North America went to Humphrey Gilbert. He died looking for the north-west passage in 1583. Elizabeth I then made Walter Raleigh – a favourite of hers and a cousin of Gilbert – the only Englishman who could organize North American expeditions.

When the colonists arrived at their new home they were often sick from the long and difficult journey. They had to make everything they needed – homes, clothes, food, drink. Often they had not brought enough **supplies** with them. The seed they had brought to plant might have been eaten by rats or sprouted in the damp, dark conditions on board. The ships that had brought them were going back to England anyway. Most colonists sent someone home at once, to fetch the things they needed.

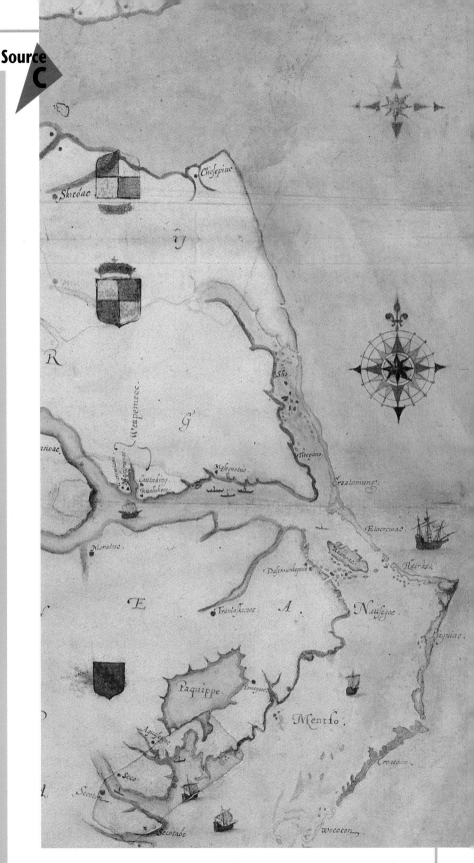

A map of Virginia, drawn in 1585 by John White, the artist who went on all the Roanoke voyages and was made Governor of the 1587 expedition. Roanoke, called 'Roanoac', is the island between the string of islands and the coast.

The first settlers

In April 1585, about 600 people left England to set up the first Roanoke colony. The colonists had orders not to harm Indians. Manteo and Wanchese taught some of them the language. But they took about 300 soldiers, and a soldier, Ralph Lane, was put in charge of the colony.

The first thing the soldiers did was build a fort. It seems clear from the **privateering** on the way to Roanoke (they captured Dutch, French and Spanish ships) that the colony was to be a privateering base, not just a farming settlement. The soldiers and the fort may have been meant as protection against the Spanish, not the Indians. But would the Indians realize that?

Relations with the Indians

To begin with, the Indians and the settlers were friends. It seemed safe to stay. The ships returned to England for supplies. The settlers had to rely on the Indians for food. The Indians happily traded food for other things. Then Lane and his men started to take what they wanted by force. No one could stop them.

Relations with the Indians got worse. Neither side trusted the other. They fought and the Indian chief was killed. The supply ships did not return. When Francis Drake called at Roanoke with supplies in June 1586 the settlers left with him. About a week later the first supply ship arrived.

Source D

When they first saw us the people ran away howling with fear like wild beasts. But we called them gently back and gave them glasses, knives, dolls and other things. Then they welcomed us, and took us to the Island of Roanoke.

Thomas Hariot, one of the settlers who had learned the Indians' language, wrote this on his return from Virginia. This was one of the first contacts with the Indians, and was friendly.

Source E

The savages made us a weir for fish and sowed corn for us. Yet until the harvest or supplies came from England we would starve if they did not help us. They and other Indians did plot against us. They would not trade, and set fire to the houses around the fort. Then we heard that there would be another attack, so I went to seize their canoes, so they could not get at us, but fighting broke out, and their chief was killed.

Part of Ralph Lane's description of events at Roanoke, written after his return. He was keen to excuse himself from having disobeyed orders by blaming the Indians.

The manner of their fishing.

Indians fishing, painted by John White in 1585. White was sent to draw and study the Indians and he seemed to get on well with them. His pictures show the Indians living a peaceful life.

Another mistake

The supply ship brought more ships (some captured by privateering on the way), supplies and more settlers. Despite the fact there had obviously been problems with the Indians, Richard Grenville, the leader of the expedition, decided to leave just eighteen men behind. He then sailed back to England. New plans for settling Virginia were made.

A new start?

In 1587 John White set out again for Roanoke, this time as governor of the expedition. His orders were to visit Roanoke and leave supplies, then set up a new colony on the Chesapeake Bay, further along the coast. Roanoke was to be a military base only.

White was determined that this time there would be peaceful settlement. He took families for the first time – 84 men, seventeen women and eleven children. Among them were his daughter, who was pregnant, and her husband.

White wanted to go straight to Roanoke without privateering along the way. But the captain and crews of the ships expected to be able to capture other ships. It was their main reason for going. White and the captain squabbled all the way to Roanoke. When they arrived the captain refused to take them further, to the Chesapeake Bay. He forced them to land at Roanoke.

The Roanoke voyages

This chart shows when people sailed for Roanoke. It was important to sail by the end of April at the latest. This was so the ships were not caught in the bad winter storms when they were going home after delivering the settlers.

Year	Who went and why
1584	First expedition to see what was there.
1585	First attempt to set up a colony: 300 settlers, 300 soldiers. Indians friendly at first. Soldiers take food by force. Indians become angry. Fighting breaks out. Settlers leave with Drake. Supplies arrive, eighteen soldiers left behind.
1587	Second attempt to set up a colony: 112 settlers. No soldiers. Forced to land at Roanoke, not the new site on the Chesapeake Bay. White sent back for supplies.
1588	White fails to get back with supplies.
1589	Expedition prepared, but not ready in time.
1590	White sails to Roanoke. with supplies. The ships' captains refuse to take any more settlers. White arrives at Roanoke to find it deserted.

Pomeiock,
an Indian village
painted by John White in 1585.

Old problems

White could not make a new start in a new place. Almost at once the Indians attacked. A settler was killed. White went to Croatoan Island, where the Indians, led by Manteo, were still friendly to White. White asked them to tell the other Indians that the settlers were peaceful. Manteo promised to try.

Nothing came of it. White's friendship with Manteo was one of the few things stopping the Indians attacking in large numbers. Despite this the settlers made White go back to England for supplies. We do not know why. On 27 August he left the settlers and his family. He would never see them again.

Source H

22 July: We went ashore where our men had been left. We found no sign of them but the bones of one the savages had killed long before.
28 July: George Howe was killed by savages who came to Roanoke either to spy on us or to hunt. They found him wading in the water, alone, unarmed except for a small forked stick which he was catching crabs with. He was shot with sixteen arrows then killed with wooden swords. After this they beat his head into pieces.

Part of John White's story of setting up the 1587 colony. From the start it was clear that there was no trust between the settlers and the Indians.

Problems at home

White returned home in September to find that there was talk of a Spanish fleet being prepared to invade England. He tried to organize supplies for the colonists. But the government was worried about England, not Roanoke. The colony had been seen as a way to attack the Spanish in America – now it was unimportant. It had been hard to set up, and the Indians were so much of a problem that no harm had been done to the Spanish. Early in October the **Privy Council** banned all ships from leaving English ports.

Getting away

Walter Raleigh and Richard Grenville, who had set up the first colony, felt responsible for the colonists. Despite the ban on ships leaving they got ships ready with supplies and extra colonists. The Privy Council sent a letter forbidding them to set out. After some pleading, the Privy Council changed their minds. They said the two smallest boats could go. So, on 22 April 1588 two ships set out, loaded with supplies and about ten new colonists.

Caught!

To his horror, White came up against the old problem. The captains of the ships wanted to privateer along the way, and took no notice of his pleadings to head straight for the colony. At first the privateering was successful. Then disaster struck.

White's ship was privateered by a French ship. It was damaged, many of the crew and passengers were hurt and all the supplies were taken. The ship had to return home. It was impossible to re-equip in time. Ships had to leave England by the end of April at the latest to avoid getting caught in the bad winter storms on the way home.

Source 1

On 6 May the French ship closed in. There was fighting on both ships that lasted about an hour and a half. There were about 23 hurt or killed on both sides, the fighting was so hard that some men had 10 or 20 wounds.

They robbed us of all our supplies, gunpowder, weapons and food, leaving us just enough biscuit to get back to England. I was wounded in the head and shot in the buttock too. Three of the **planters** were hurt and the ship's Master and Mate.

We were forced to return to England. This was a punishment from God for earlier thievery.

Part of John White's story of the 1588 voyage to Virginia. It is clear that he was very much against privateering, which he calls thievery, despite the fact that it was generally accepted as a normal thing to do.

A painting of the battle of Gravelines, when the Armada broke up. Preparations for the Armada, and problems after, seriously delayed sending help to the Roanoke colony.

The Armada

Now even Raleigh and Grenville were too busy to help the colonists because the Armada came and was driven off. Everyone celebrated. It was too late to send ships to Roanoke.

Yet another mistake

Raleigh and Grenville organized another expedition. It was not ready by April 1589. They could have sent one supply ship, but not all of them. For some reason, we do not know why, they decided to wait.

White did not set out for Roanoke again until the spring of 1590. When he did leave it was with privateers who would not take many supplies or any new settlers. Helping the colony was not the main aim of the voyage. White was not in charge of the expedition, the privateers were.

The Spanish Armada

Philip II of Spain was a Catholic. Elizabeth was a Protestant. At first Philip kept on good terms with England. He even asked Elizabeth to marry him. But it became clear that she would not marry him. She even helped his Protestant enemies. She allowed English sailors to raid his treasure ships in the Indies. She let Drake raid Spain itself. The last straw was when Elizabeth executed her Catholic cousin, Mary Queen of Scots. Philip got a huge fleet (the Armada) ready. He wanted it to invade England and make it a Catholic country, ruled from Spain. He was so sure he would win that the nobles he wanted to rule England were on the ships, ready to take over. But the Armada failed.

Gone!

White once more had to wait to reach Roanoke until the privateers were satisfied with their raids. But at last, after a skirmish with the Spanish, Roanoke was sighted. There was a column of smoke coming from roughly the right direction. A smaller ship navigated its way into the shallow water between the string of islands and the shore. On 18 August 1590, nearly three years after he left, White was back.

The settlers were all gone. The fire was just some grass burning. There were no signs that the colony had been attacked by Indians, as there had been in 1587. The houses had been carefully taken down, as if to use in another place. There were no skeletons. But there were no people either and there were signs of a quick departure. Among the things that White found were his three chests of possessions, dug up and opened. There was a large shelter with the word CROATOAN (the name of the island that Manteo's Indians lived on) carved on a post by the entrance.

The last straw

White convinced himself that the colonists, including his family, were safe at Croatoan. He arranged to sail there the next day. But there was very bad weather. One of the ships was damaged. The captain decided to go back to England. White, on the other ship, waited for the wind to change to sail to Croatoan. It did not change. The captain said they were too low on food, it was too late in the year and the weather was too bad to stay any longer. They returned to England. White could not get anyone else interested in another expedition. Raleigh was caught up in **Court** politics and by 1592 he was in the Tower of London.

White went to live in Ireland. In 1593 he wrote to a friend saying that he wished things had turned out differently, but he had to 'commit the relief of my company of planters to the merciful help of God'. This is the last we know about him or the colony.

Source K

We fired our guns near the shore and blew our trumpets and sang familiar English songs, but we had no answer.

We came to where I left our colony in 1587. The houses had been taken down. We found five chests broken into that had been hidden by the planters. Three were mine. Many of my things lay about the place spoiled and broken.

My books were torn from the covers, my maps and pictures torn from their frames and spoiled by the rain. My armour was almost eaten through with rust. The savages must have dug them up after our people left for Croatoan. I was sad to lose my things, but overjoyed that they (the people) were safe.

Part of John White's story of the 1590 voyage to Virginia.

This detail from John White's map of Virginia shows the mainland, Roanoke and Croatoan.

What happened?

We do not know what happened to the colonists. If they went to Croatoan there is no evidence to prove it. If they went inland or up the coast towards the Chesapeake Bay (where they had first meant to settle) there is no evidence of that, either. Their bodies were never found in excavations that were made in the Roanoke area. They could have been carried off by the Indians and killed somewhere else. They could have gone to live with various Indian groups. They could have built a village somewhere else, that eventually failed and has not yet been found.

GLOSSARY

caravels ships used for exploration because they were small, light (weighing 100 tons), fast and easy to steer

carracks ships used for trading because they were large, heavy (weighing 1,000 tons), and could carry a lot of cargo

Catholic a Christian who accepts the Pope as head of the Church

Christian a person who believes that Jesus Christ was the son of God and who tries to follow his teachings

cinnamon the inside bark of the cinnamon tree, dried in the sun and used as a spice for flavouring food

colony a group of people from one country living in another country that belongs to the country they come from

donkey train a group of people with donkeys loaded with goods, travelling together for safety from attack

disease sickness

fort a building designed to keep the people inside (most often soldiers) safe from any attack

hides the skins of animals

Indies China and Asia

lice insect that lives in human hair and bites humans to feed on their blood

maggots the stage that a fly goes through after it has been an egg and before it becomes a fly. Maggots live on rotting food or plants.

merchant a person who buys and sells things

military base a place with a fort and soldiers, set up to defend a friendly area, or to make attacks on land or ships owned by the enemy

mines places where precious metals or minerals are dug out of the ground

monarch a king or queen

MP a Member of Parliament: a person who represents a particular area of the country in Parliament

Muslim a person who follows the Islamic religion. They believe in one God, Allah, and the teachings of a prophet called Mohammad.

mutiny a rebellion against whoever is in charge. Used mostly for rebellions in the army or navy, when the ordinary soldiers or sailors rebel against an officer.

native the local inhabitants of a country

Henry VII	Henry VIII
1485	1509

30

navigator a person who guided ships across the sea, using maps, sea charts and the stars

noble a person who comes from an important family

pilot a local person who guided ships up rivers and into harbours which are difficult and which the pilot knows well

planters a word used at the time to refer to people who went to set up colonies

Pope the Head of the Roman Catholic Church. All Catholics, no matter what country they lived in, had to obey the Pope. If the Pope and the monarch of a country wanted different things, Catholics were supposed to obey the Pope.

privateering attacking ships from another country at sea and stealing the ship and anything it was carrying

Privy Council people, usually nobles, chosen by the monarch to give advice about running the country

provisions things that a person needs – especially used about food

ransom money demanded for the release of a person or property that has been captured

scurvy condition caused by lack of vitamin C. It causes bleeding gums and the person feels tired, sick and weak.

slave a person who is owned by another person and is forced to work for them

supplies stores of anything that people need – food, weapons, tools or cloth

trade buying and selling things

vitamin C something the body needs to keep healthy. It is found in fresh fruit and vegetables.

voyages journeys, especially by ship

weevils long-headed beetles that eat grain, nuts and food made from these things (like bread and biscuits)

> **Money**
> 12 pence (d) in a shilling (s)
> 20 shillings (s) in a pound (£)

Edward VI	Mary I	Elizabeth I
47	1553	1558	1603

INDEX